HAND & SKULL

Zoë Brigley (Thompson) grew up in Caerphilly in the Rhymney Valley of Wales, and is now an Assistant Professor at the Ohio State University in the US. She won an Eric Gregory Award in 2003 and received a Welsh Academy bursary in 2005. All three of her collections, published by Bloodaxe, are Poetry Book Society Recommendations. Her debut, *The Secret* (2007), was longlisted for the Dylan Thomas Prize in 2008, and was followed by *Conquest* (2012) and *Hand & Skull* (2019).

A book of her non-fiction essays, *Notes from a Swing State*, is due from Parthian Books in 2019. She also researches violence against women, and is co-editor of a volume of scholarly essays, *Feminism, Literature and Rape Narratives* (Routledge, 2010).

ZOË BRIGLEY
HAND & SKULL

IMAGES BY
VICTORIA BROOKLAND
ALFRED STIEGLITZ

BLOODAXE BOOKS

Poems copyright © Zoë Brigley 2019
Artwork © Victoria Brookland 2019
Alfred Stieglitz photograph: see page 70

ISBN: 978 1 85224 472 7

First published 2019 by
Bloodaxe Books Ltd,
Eastburn,
South Park,
Hexham,
Northumberland NE46 1BS.

www.bloodaxebooks.com
For further information about Bloodaxe titles
please visit our website and join our mailing list
or write to the above address for a catalogue.

Supported by
**ARTS COUNCIL
ENGLAND**

Cover design: Neil Astley & Pamela Robertson-Pearce.

Printed in Great Britain by Bell & Bain Limited, Glasgow, Scotland, on
acid-free paper sourced from mills with FSC chain of custody certification.

That skull had a tongue in it and could sing once.

SHAKESPEARE

You knew; you understood; you felt the world outside tugging
with all its golden hands.

EDITH WHARTON

CONTENTS

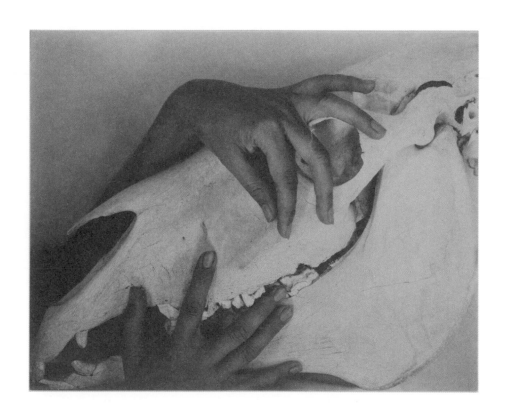

ALFRED STIEGLITZ: 'GEORGIA O'KEEFFE, HANDS AND HORSE SKULL' (1931)

Blind Horse Elegy

Go after him and tell him we will give a sound horse for each
that was maimed. And tell him what kind of man did it, a man
of my mother's blood, who I cannot kill or destroy.

The Second Branch of the Mabinogi

Almost as soon as they are born, they
begin to run: the teeth in their heads
take more space than their brains,
and the eyes are the largest of all.
The mare is walking a rope around
the paddock: stamping in place: sour
muscles taut: stretched under hide:
horse stench steaming from her mane.
You didn't know how big her eyes
were when you read

the Welsh tale: *Ac yn hynny guan y dan
y meirych, a thorri y guefleu wrth y
danned udunt, a'r clusteu wrth y penneu:*
how rather than let his sister have
them (those high horses) he took
a box cutter to their lips, clipped ears
from heads, and where he could hold
them, slit their eyelids to bone. When
you talk of a horse running

perhaps you mean that as a child, you
loved your long-legged ease: the way
skin freckled with the trees:
somersaulting hills: a harras of
horses synchronous as legs: bending
and straightening in flight. How
sometimes you have ridden them:
urged them faster: thighs moving
against them: hips thrown up:
clutching. He would

cut off their tails high to the spine,
hack at their forelocks so the skin of
the forehead slips, would treat them
just as shamefully as he knows how.
Except leave them alive—still just
alive. If the tortured were blind,
there would be nothing to see: the crowd
gathered because it wanted to
watch them gurn: a*y*

yuelly y gwnaethant wy am uorwyn cystal
a honno? Frozen in the grass you
found an albino crow, and tried
to pick it up with gloves and trowel:
it took to its legs: half-flew into the
bush. They named you Harmless.
In a hundred years, there'll be no more
wild horses, not even on the steppes, but
tonight, with a bread knife,

he plans to carve your tail. *I will*
punish you all for it. I'll take great
pleasure in it. The crew is arriving:
the barn on fire: a last pale dawn
froths in the horse's eye.

Poem for Emily Doe

The next thing
she remembers, she is on a gurney
in a hallway. She has dried blood
and bandages on the backs
of her hands and elbow. She thinks,
maybe I have fallen. She is very
calm. She signs
the papers. Three nurses
prise flora and fauna
from her hair. Pine needles scratch
the back of her neck. She
shuffles from room to room
with a blanket wrapped
around, needles trailing
behind: she leaves a little pile
in every room she sits in—

Undressing Poem

he forces her tiny shirt buttons out of each
slot, though they wedge in place & it takes
the pressure of a finger—the countering
thumb to budge each one

Letter from Georgia O'Keeffe

He opened the lens – and I did as I was told –
sat long and bare for the stretch of a four-minute
exposure. A stormy night on Lake George – and later
he wrote – *All is right between us for you gave me*
your virginity. You offered the very center. And he hung
me in pieces on his gallery wall. He is – I suspect
– always photographing himself. Where I saw

a tree with a cut limb – in pain but lovely
and live – he cropped a dying chestnut
crying with a man's soul. When I knew the hot
moon and its reflection – white and mingling
on the waves – he mapped a line between land
and sky – and the moon watching

passive. Every part of me he saw in fragments. *Bits*
of universality in a woman's body. Neck. Torso.
Breasts. People often say funny things about
my hands. How admired they have been
when painting – smeared as they are – but preferable
to the white, useless hands men know

so well. He had me boxed – until
my leaving – when he accused me – for
I went on – no longer a pet or creature – not his
Georgia O'Keeffe. I walked out naked
onto the long sigh of the land under
a darkening sky. As good a place as any –
I told him – to let your bones bleach.

Poem on the Edge

I was trying / to explain

    I said / *Once there was this / photograph of me / taken by a man / I loved / it was a Polaroid / the bathroom / lit by two / candles though you only see one / in the frame it was night / rain trip-trapped / on the roof there was a moaning / sound at times / branches thumped against / the shutters of the house*

    You said / *Well what about / it?*

    I said / *It's someone / else in the photograph...*

    You said / *Is that / all? It's such / a cliché you know / your younger self being / another person and all that / just a dull / idea I'd forget / if I were you and write / about something / else*

    You spoke / kindly almost / fatherly but / where once was space / opening a bloom / entering the lungs now / was nothing not / even a sigh

    I couldn't speak / to you then but / I'm telling you / now it is all / true / the bathroom the wind / candles and rain but / here's what else

    It is the moment before / something terrible happens / she is alone in the house with / this man taking / the photograph she / is lying naked / in the bathtub he is leaning / over impossible to / pass so she just / lies still refuses / to look eyes down / away the photo taken / from above framing / from the long fair / hair on her head / to the soft brown / hair between / her legs / her lower-arms covered / by water as if cased / in glittering sleeves her fingers / reach out of the water to / pluck from the bath a string / of miraculous / handkerchiefs young / breasts falling / mouth tensed for / a blow

    I wish I could / have told you but / you would not / have understood how hard / it was looking through / the man with the camera / what beauty he made / of tautness / the fear of / the girl on / the edge / long and waiting

Letter on a Sheep Skull

On top of the mountain where I grew
up were two farms, each loathing
the other. At first, there were simply rumours:
poison in the animal feed; a sheep's

head on the farmer's drive, severed
and tossed. One night I woke to an uneasy
glow: the farm on fire, and people came
from miles around, carrying flasks

or picnics, but all climbing barbed wire
to watch the barn burn until dawn.
They just stood there, looking as if
it were happening behind

glass: a gaze not cruel but without
pity. Farms fall away—the abandoned dairies
where I walked the collie, moss leeching
the stone blocks where silver churns

lined up for delivery. Behind the farm gate
was another life I gathered. A sheep draining
red and black rivulets in the lane, later its skull
picked yellow and clean. Or the lamb

we found dying in spring
snow. I covered the newborn
thing with my coat, but the mother
ewe tore it away

with her teeth. I cried
to the poor creatures, to the lamb
blundering close, to wool shivering
in clumps on the sharp side of the wire.

Dryad

I gave her what she asked: had she asked more
I would have given it.

He is behind you now. He bites,
snatches away. He embraces your face
and fists. The incline of your dress
blown back; branches pressed by his hands.

You think of the others: Syrinx,
the reed-woman, transformed into
a mournful sound; Pitys turned to pine,
rocked by the North Wind; and Daphne

who was at her end a sweet laurel.
We are all who have pleased too well.
Shouldn't hurt... The bark of a prayer.
He almost has you. Now he's sure

that you're caught. The gale

                 blows through
                      the branches,
           your tumbling hair.

Dressing Poem

the comb in her hair becomes
a centipede & her compact
a turtle shell & the brush
for powder a great soft
broom & the glass
a fish bowl flashing

Sonnet for the Hole in the Glass

You know the women through every manmade thing
that men have used to trap them: a van's double doors
closing: a keyboard: letters lined up like crows
on telephone wires: barbs on a fence: a door that opens
to a queue of men: at night stepping onto a white bus:
that moment on the edge of what is about to happen.
In a cell, they choose between sex or jail: the cop car
where they apologise: *Thank you, Sir, thank you for not
booking me tonight:* the papers they sign from hospital
gurneys: or the shiny, blue cellphone light that hooks
them onscreen like tiny, pink fish. Punch a hole
in the glass: cracks spidering: ice too thin to carry
the weight of men: one eye to the gap just
wide enough for you to read their names.

Letter from Tess Durbeyfield

I am always brave
on long walks home: the wet lane: tender steps over
waters which break the gully banks, and cross
the path in shiny, grey fingers: ribbons
lacing. I walk, even when
stretches of land open like an empty
stomach. The chestnut trees were lopped one
by one to stumps: first platforms for children to raise
fists and clamour, later nothing but a dull spot
amongst the sharper green. I pass, and
by the knobbly hesitation of my limbs, by my straight,
pretty body, and the bright swing
of my hair, I know myself exactly. I feel myself
blank and longing under my schoolgirl coat.
No one could know how I hate it. In my pocket,
chestnuts the colour of hide, the shade
of a thoroughbred, though marred
by a spot of white that might
be an eye or navel. I don't know
it now, but I am about
to bend. The snap of a branch, or bone
under a human hand.

Forgetting Poem

If you had to choose between remembering everything or nothing at all,
which would you pick?

Something happened, because a man
you cared about came into your house
at night, or because in the stories

you read, men were *gracious* and *kind*,
had a woman's *best interests* at heart.
If you could forget all the things

                              you've done...the deck on the ferry
                              at Dover when the dawn light flamed
                              the chalk: green uniforms waiting

                    for bribes on the other side: a motorboat on
                    the brown Usumacinta River: the sickening
                    pitch of the boat as it rounded Ramsey Island:

                    brown seals plunging in foam: and the whale
                              glistening, suspended in its lurch
                              from the water. How happy you were

                    with your cousins at Deia: small hands
                    clasping the edge of your sweater, pinching
                    the cotton of your skirt: when the hardest

                              decision of the day was the angle
                              of a chair: how far to stretch
                                                      into sun

or shadow.
A woman flew out to meet her rapist, a man
from another country, absent for years.

How liberating, she said, *to forgive*
and forget. But what if your rapist is not
a handsome man in a collarless shirt, not

close to tears or poised to make it
up as best he can? What if mercy isn't asked for
and cannot be given? A bell swung,

                             never pealing: in fairy tales, the princess
                           breathes in the blue rose, and forgets
                    it all: the voyage by sea: the storm: *not even*

               my name. She forgets the boy: a clambering
          spider on the arm of a giant—only the rose—and
             a lover she won't remember is washed up

            on a beach somewhere. By the same ocean but
           a continent away, you dusted the boardwalks
                with the soles of your feet: dipped

                a hand in the warm, brown mouth
                    of the lily ponds: took off
               your clothes for the cold, stark slip

          to saltwater: or the white porcelain of a bathtub,
            where your body lay: the length of the white
         tiled room: a window cracked on a blue rectangle

               of sky: powdered vanilla that you carried
           on your skin as you travelled: blackberry jam
                 on your tongue for summer holidays

in England
on a small,
square lawn.

You didn't know when you began what
happiness was, so you missed it when
it appeared. Now you are talking about

> some kind of freedom. Because you're afraid,
> at your worst, you're still blundering
> with the key to door: a man beside

> you, perhaps not yet knowing what
> he is about to do: a starling flew up
> from the garden's end, its wings rustling

like newspaper among the brambles.
Sorry, it said. *I am so very*
sorry.

VICTORIA BROOKLAND: 'HORSE'

Letter to a Horse's Head

I first surmised the horse's heads
Were toward Eternity—

EMILY DICKINSON

Teens commit suicide in my hometown: 25
dead, no older than 19. They hang
from ceiling lights and branches. *Nothing to do*

here—nothing—but maybe go out at night
and get drunk. The played-out bars: The Woodland,
The Star, not to mention the clubs where if

you have the money and can stand up,
they'll serve you. Everyone's there: hopers, no-hopers;
rugby players at Mollies, thighs squeezed into slim skirts.

We were all vandals; I was with them, laughing
or snapping at passers-by, our mouths sprung,
but our grandparents knew that what ripens falls,

fails. We ride the Mari Lwyd, star-horse of the frost,
her cranium stripped to yellow bone. Her head
lurches on a stick from house to house:

stubs of broken bottles make eyes
in her empty sockets, coloured ribbons
from her skull, and a coin in her jaw.

Now oak leaves flame the stumps, the spat
stone teeth of the foundries, where
in heat and joy, we cheer to the night:

I come with a rope around my neck to save you.

Poem with a Least Favourite Dress

In this place and occasion I represent a woman, and in all respects
I ought to represent her as faithfully as I can.
EDWARD HYDE, New York Assembly 1702

so heavy & she hardly wore it because the colour
was near but not close enough to a browner shade
the only consolation the sheen the dress had on winter
mornings or boat rides on a smooth grey lake
a horse's chestnut hide glinting bronze and green

Revolver

(after Alun Lewis 1915-1944)

When I asked how you died, all they could say
was no one was sure if the pistol discharged
by accident when the body fell. You didn't die
in Goppe Pass, but lay for six hours on stretchers,

a hospital cot. That last time you said goodbye,
you imagined a homecoming, somewhere imperials and snobs
hadn't spoiled, where you stepped across the lawn in wet
shoes. What thought before the moment

closed? Gratitude? Or fear tugging the thread, unravelling
sleeves, yielding skirts? Or bliss, that day
on a motorcycle rumbling due north over the Sahyadri?
Rain that fell on the tents of soldiers, falls now

on me, possesses me entirely. If you were alive, I'd say
that I read your letters, and like the others,
I was almost in love. The only one that can tell is
the revolver itself: one empty case and five live rounds.

Western Union

Here's a story—not mine—of a woman out West,
not the American West as it is now, but

a place without time. Long ago, she shed her dress,
and now she wears a belt and boots, faces the men

round the campfire. Like Claudia Cardinale or
Katy Jurado in a film I once saw: *Nothing*

you can do to me, not a thing, that won't wash off
with soap and water. One man watches, and does

nothing. Another one behind her, encircling
with one arm: the other hand stabs, slices her open

from sternum to navel. She gasps at the wound:
not guts, but wire, pistons, circuits. Did you see

it too? The moment that told us what violation
meant: forced to look, to see nothing like flesh.

Poem with Whalebone Crinoline

bones fan out to expand from a flat
cage: opening like an accordion's bellow, but without
the sound, & when the skirt drapes
over, a space round the waist
is wide enough to tempt
a woman or man to reach across

The Eye in the Wall

O sweet and lovely wall,
Show me thy chink, to blink through with mine eyne!

At her house on the hill, he was meant to drop
her off, but followed her to the door, where
she leaned for a minute before fumbling
with the key. That was before the sex began.
He loved her fifteen-year-old pleasure, how easy
it was to make her come, but he couldn't find

his own without hurting her. Like looking
through a hole in the wall, he thinks of her again,
wonders if it was wrong, assures himself it was
right. He still has the photo he took when
he tied her to the legs of table. Like setting his eye
to a crack, but she cannot see him, doesn't know

he is there. That time in the pine forest, she faced
him under a moonless, cloudy evening, at the edge
of frosted needles, near the brightly lit windows
of a small brick house: he wanted to fuck her where
children might look out at any moment, wanted
to fuck her nastily like his fat father fucked

his thin mother. He could have been a nurse
or a geologist, could have cared for animals
or the elderly. He knows he is kind, compassionate
by nature, so years later, he writes, the words
squirming from the email to tell her: *Sometimes
I sit quietly and try to remember on long journeys home, or
sometimes at work. On evening drives, I often think of you.*

The Shave

That night, he nailed her plaits to the floor,
split the dull cotton of her skirt and vest
to shave away the coppery threads.

The hair wound around his lithe left hand:
his right held a blade—snip-snap at the best
of her golden head and off it came on the bed-sheets.

The severed hair spelled a ladder
with rungs that could carry a man.
Poor little oyster, shucked

gristle, jellied and spat out
food, she had nothing
to keep him, and nothing besides.

Hand & Breast

'We flatter &

embarrass—but—

because we have faith—we dare to

record what is far too intimate.'

Post Colonial

She couldn't blame the place where
it happened. The mountain, a blind
animal, innocent as any massive herbivore:
purple with heather in spring; red with dying
fern in the autumn; stark and bald in the snow.
It wasn't the fault of the town, spokes of roads
leading out and away: like the city but poorer
and more desperate. An outpost of the marches
in the old days, wood huts leaned against
the castle walls, later drowned by a moat, or
dwarfed under towers that tilted to lean by
English cannon. How could she blame
a town built to conquer and maim. She doesn't

go back often, but when she does, it's a place
she's passing through. It wasn't because
the place was poor: in every town, men follow
behind from school, eyes on a girl's shape
all the way: in every school when you tell
your teacher, they'll ask if one is your boyfriend.
She likes to think that if she'd lived up the valley,
none of it would have happened; that in the village
where her family lived for a hundred years,
poor as it was, she would have been safe.
Not the place itself, but the jobless towns heaved
to life: spaces between: the gaps that swallow
without mercy, without pity, without grace.

Beatitudes for the Women

1 the officers you know are not here / to serve they come to get served /
walking is soliciting every night / in the alley they ask / you to "choose" /
their eyes on you now / examining what is hidden / whether under your
dress / is a staircase / for them to climb

2 a judge in Bolton / England rejects the case of / you in the chat-room a
woman / who typed *I would love to try* / *group sex* words lifting / from screen
to the brain / of a listener who skewed / your fantasy to his instructions
/ setting out on the drive to your online lover's / how light and bold /
you felt but how sharp / the plunge when / the door opened and you saw
/ *them* not the one lover / you were promised but / a queue lining up

3 what should you say / stepping away from / a face feverish white / his
blue uniform / undone? not worse than dying / despite the old saying but
/ still fear / a shot in the back / so the one / thing you utter is *Thank* /
you, sir. Thank you

4 not long afterwards a man took / photographs / one of you / in the stark
light of the bathroom your hair / tied and face looking / at white tile /
when you couldn't / see the portrait / you tore into pieces / you did not
know / what violation meant but you carried / it around / glowing / like
the picture he kept

5 leaving the cinema / you walk from / the foyer to the night / outside
and you might be thinking / of a tiger and boy on a raft / on film a
human tooth / in a flower and you ask your friend / if the hyena was
meant to symbolise / the cannibal cook or if the boy was the tiger / all
along humans carnivorous / but at the stop a white / bus is waiting / a
boy by the wheel calling / hurrying you now to step / onboard lightly on
the edge / of what is about to happen

6 the lover who / made your womb a room / he wanted for him alone /
and it kept him / awake / the red-walled stain / left behind by other / men

7 if you said yes once then why not / sleep with one more / is what they would argue / later in court in front / of the jurors lawyers / witnesses all were told / you woke alone in the suite / nothing to recall but / a smudge of faces pressed / against the window the clank / of the fire escape and you / under the shiny blue / light of a cellphone / you onscreen / like a tiny fish

Poem with Seams

the little grooves pressed from seams onto skin: hardly

perceptible: lines crossing: pinking the flesh: present like

a fingertip against a forehead or chin: its small, insistent presence

VICTORIA BROOKLAND: VÉSUVIENNES

Letter to Leda on Getting Married

Women must destroy in themselves the desire to be loved.
MINA LOY

I'll remember your bridal gown that isn't
white, but will not remember the other
man from before that we both
loved in our own way. I'll remember the bulls
lowing at dawn and the milk-cows lulling
together. I will not remember you
flirting with the Spaniard at the market.
I'll remember the altar, a window

to the hills where you are blessed. I won't
remember my baby on the blanket coughing
up twigs in milky sick, or the toddler who bit
the nose of the flower girl. I try not
to remember what you said, stood by
the water: promises shrieked on the night
estuary. I'll forget you said you still
weren't sure. Leda, sometimes you come

in dreams: a great white bird blooming
on the lake. I know I should tell you to forget
the past, but remember too. I must not say
that it isn't enough to want children.
Leda, you are not me, and when I kiss you
goodbye, I remember not to be selfish.
Now you are stepping up like a goddess:
now you are walking out into the light.

Poem with a Wedding Dress

the folds were winged
but narrow as a hawk, fringes
like horse mane, a dress that blotted
the day, but cathedral tall, its skirts in full sail

Swan

I see you then: long and veined with red like the closed
pod of an asphodel bud: if you opened now it would be

with the strangeness of a lily its scent edging between sweat,
and the musk that marks a territory: I did not forget you:

in the bed my other children are sleeping: they climb
under the covers: a fluffed head on my shoulder: tiny

toes cold against my leg: in the morning light, the children
might shake themselves to feathers and float away: I will find

them pale and half-transformed: one arm becomes a great
white wing: at the end of the leg a black, webbed swan-foot:

nothing could be happier than finding them whole: tides drag
to the land and back again: cool night: the children wake

to the red of closed eyelids: strings are trilling or snapping
loose from their pegs: the wet stamen of lilies offer

themselves up to the bees: fear spinning: if I knitted a nightshirt
of nettle leaves, you would not be a swan flying away.

Rare

(after Georgia O'Keeffe)

Men make of me some strange unearthly creature
breathing in clouds for nourishment, but the truth
is that I like beefsteak, and I like it rare at that.

No squeamishness when the meat is tenderised.
No sentiment allowed for the dull face of the cow
with its long lashes, the mother and her calf-love,

and the baby itself when it is born, dainty hooves
emerging from the cow's rear, the head wet
with blood, eyes closed, ears flat and forlorn

at its entrance. Some creatures are eaters, others
are eaten, but only a set of sharp teeth will make
me, not a creature, but a human being.

Syringe

When any man puts his mouth to you, he draws out the scale
of love and dread: misted breath from wet lips on an icy
day, or exhausted fog from the mouth of a smoker: charred
winters, crouched on the fire escape in the back alley. So long

since the summer at the marsh when you walked the boardwalk
alone, the bluebottles so lazy they would not stop jolting
bare arms and shoulders, wings zipping and whirring: each
a tiny electric shock. You stood watching the reeds:

their spear points spinning or rising: dots of static between
TV channels: sometimes dipping: bowing a waltz: each thinking
blade knowing the others: each move with the grace
of numbers. You are swallowing, gulping pebbles to rattle

in an empty place: hollow needle: like Syrinx, the reed-woman,
you make yourself spiked and narrow, speaking only when
the wind blows through you, spun back to what happened
so long before in some small town, one indifferent summer.

Round Trip

A box full of scissors: knives: hair clips
at the airport. Amsterdam bell gables:
Italian step gables: a long building
with wide windows and above it

the mountains. But that was only
a picture pasted in the lid
of a cigar box. MARIETTA in gold
letters and inside in a row

lay ten cigars like pupae
poised to collapse: birthing smoke
wings over the heavy rot of the British
canal. Now the water

freezes: stillness: a country out
there on the ice with stranded pieces
of wood: a lost ball. Pitted surface of the road
pocked: bedded by chippings:

we followed it home to the surprise
of mountain curves. From the farm
at bottom a car slides forward and above
a boy is poised with his bike on the slopes.

We will crack our fingers in the pond
for a piece of ice: mirrors splitting
our fists. Crows flying up without a
sound and wings tired by their slow beating.

The man who shouts across the frozen canal.
A dog tenses its back at the gate. Fingers
cold as tubers. Wooden feet. Unnatural
length of the body: longing to be wound tight.

White Patio with Red Door

I have written to you so many times
about closed courtyards, the spring
that wells up in Song of Solomon,
the garden that my grandfather
tended, where roses, their gorgeous
faces gazed over the smouldering
wreckage of cars. Only you know
that the interior place I dreamed
was a garden razed, the door split
on its hinges and gaping, and how
to shore up that small square space
enough to unfasten myself for you?

Vésuviennes

—redacted from *Only Paradoxes to Offer: French Feminists and the Rights of Man* by Joan Wallach Scott, p.80.

critics   caricaturists

                              played upon

                inversion   ugly, comical,

funny-looking, masculine   manly

    marital   children left

arms   despairing   mothers

women with monocles, cigars, and beards   men in skirts

           a man pleading   the woman barring the door

             take his pants to his wife   sew

a button on them   a man backing off

               female security

    a huge pair of scissors pointed   his crotch

Paris police   recruiting prostitutes   bogus

       Vésuviennes

              so successful in its parody

         treated as   genuine

         men who refused

       service

crossing   boundaries

                  efface the differences between

                      the limits of

modesty and ridicule   gracious form

    and good taste   men—given

their undertaker's getup—can hardly complain

Poem with a High Waist

in those Katharine Hepburn
high-waisted pants their buttons
on the side stamped with an anchor
& chain she sat
on the floor cross-legged at the ankles the long
loaves of her lace-up shoes *I've never hit anything*
she said *that was in the right place*

The Amish Roofers

When I turn the corner, they are up there:
Amish men on the roof: cool, collarless
in shirts and braces: some with beards: others
without. Most bend double wielding hammers
high, their thudding irregular against
stone or woodwork: raps skidding over each
other. A few wear straw hats: some hanging
from ladders: others crouch at the edge where
the path goes: right by the brink of the sounds,
and I try not to look when I pass, though
they gaze at me with praise or disdain. Hot
breezes gust over Tudek: long grasses
humming: buzzing at my bare legs: and blows
of Amish mallets pounding down on me.

Poem with Stockings and Suspenders

the legs lengthen in their stockings, grow a shiny
        second skin, the long seam at the back as if to say,
I know you're watching, I know what you can see

VICTORIA BROOKLAND: 'I TOO AM A RARE PATTERN'

Letter from Edna Pontellier

The beginning and end stretched so far
away, to motionless blue sails, the meadow
yellow and high around my hips. I threw
out my arms when I walked, like swimming,
sometimes striking my tall waist, hands
beating tips of the long grass. I could
have walked on forever, without ever
leaving the green. I was running away
for a stretch from the Presbyterian close.

As a child, they called me a little gloom.
Did he think I was afraid? Why didn't he
come? Don't mind what I'm saying: I am
just thinking aloud under a white shawl.
I could tell you that I love how he closes
his brows, and his eye is a little out;
how he has a square lip, a chin he can't
straighten. I found the old swimsuit still
hanging on its peg, and there alone

beside the bathhouse, in a soft, close body,
I cast away the pricking grass. I was a newborn
wave, opening its eye in a familiar face
that it had never known. The foamy world
curled up to its white wavelets, coiled
creatures about my feet; it reached
out with a long, sweeping arm: like the sea
where I swam out in gray fear, believing
there would be no meadow and no child.

Star / Sun / Snow

I *Star*

You were the second. Small in the womb,
kept alive on whispers and songs, nights
spent rocking in the chair, days at the doctor's
listening to your heart beating. You were born
in the Fall. I lay awake through the wee hours
as you spasmed inside. Your father drove us
to the hospital, and it was all
red: sky, leaves, and pavement: your
head a pointed star trapped
by my pelvic bone, but they trimmed, sliced,
opened me up, and out you came screaming,
slippery with my blood. No apology,
but a pause as you laid your head
on my stomach, craned your neck, and
with livid black eyes, you saw
me at last.

II *Sun*

You were the third, big and radiant
in my stomach, but you made me
nauseous at the smell of grilled cheese,
always sick from too much food,
or too little, too much sleep or not
enough. Your growing singed the edges
of my day. You were a hot thing
in snow. On the day of your birth,
I walked to the operating theatre with a cold
spine. Many hands pushed down to wrestle you out
of the abdomen. Then the nurse held you up

in the green light of the surgery. They brought
you close to my face to kiss your wet
head. I couldn't rest until the warm clutch
of you was tucked beneath
my breast.

III *Snow*

You were the first, the one not
born, seen once onscreen shivering with excitement, or
pain. After you died, they scraped
you out of me. But I don't know what they did
with what remained. Knotted in blue plastic, or combusting
from the basement incinerator, smoke hung with the first
unseasonal snow that year? Now, flakes spin,
melt on the warm earth. If you had lived, we would
have opened the door today, and I
would have said: *Look, the snowflakes are
trying to come in*, and you might have crouched
on the wooden boards, your small, round cheek almost
touching the floor, your eye so close to the snowflake, the tiny
perfection of its sharp, white symmetry. Gone by the time
I ask *Can you
see it?*

Eagle Poem

Tell Papa and Alia – if you see them – that I loved them up
to the very last moment

MARINA TSVETAEVA

I release
you rapturous in flight
young eagle
hanging eye fixed
under the sun
my looking pale
and fragile under your
blazing

Name Poem

We live to say her name.

MARIA LOFTUS in 'The Club No Parent Wants to Join',
New York Times, 29 December 2017

Your name sings a feathery thing in the hand:
a name hums like ice frosting the tongue.
On the smack of two lips, your name
is sung: spat black letters:
the satisfying flight of ball from hand to hand:
or the silver retort when clapper meets bell.

When a stone is thrown up over flat water,
the sob that breaks the surface is the song
of your name. Night hooves rapping
sound out your name, unexpected like thunder,
and intimate as a gun to the temple:
your name sounds the trigger click.

How impossible to sing your name!
This name of yours, delicate as a kiss on the eye,
lips frosting each lid, and even more
a name sung by a mouthful of snow,
blue and glacial: icy water gulped deep:
this name that sings a long drink of sleep.

Poem with a Mourning Dress

so easy & right fitting
clean clothes with your first morning dress
buttons snapped shut stockings long
& taut against your legs the seams
of your underwear matching the shape
of you a heavy necklace on your chest
is a comforting hand

Letter from Nemi

If we could perceive death as a part of pregnancy, we might just take women more seriously.

CLAUDIA DEY

Some men look at women, and see sex. You know them:
how they stare when the pregnancy shows, smiling that smile

of intimate knowledge. But how much joy there was
in the making: the rain tapping the roof with a dry

sound as if falling on paper or skin: the moon up: unlike
any other: big and blank and gilded by honey: fingering

clouds passing across: tangling hair: streamers over
a lifted face: mouth open and defiant. Out in the lake

are luxurious Roman goddesses submerged for centuries
like sunken ships *Have you seen the place of Diana's remains*

down there? So terribly overgrown, the temples filled in, a great
excavation. On the ultrasound, a foetus: so small that

the womb scans empty. You knew from childhood:
no afterlife: only blank space. Are women just a place

to put things? For men distracted by the time
on their phones, by dinner, or a train they have to catch, by

their mothers? On the terrace, he turns to you, saying:
Maggie, hold this. He puts it in your hand, and lights it:

a firecracker. It flames through your fingers before
you drop it. After eight weeks, there is some blood, and

clotted tissue, dark red and shiny like liver. You overdress
tastefully, patterned collusion brilliant against

your shiny, white dress. You picnic in the ruins at night: a flask,
bread and cheese laid out on red and white checkers.

A woman died this week in Argentina, bled out inducing
miscarriage by tablet. In the temple, stone is marbled:

blue veins in the breast of a goddess. Overhead,
the moon might be a virgin or crone: a hunter

carrying arrows and a spear: cloud of fury and teeth like
a pack of hounds: tearing the limbs of men who look its way: or

just a deer with golden antlers running away. Still you watch
the hunt: the moon orbiting close: rain pulses shame:

leaves beaten as they quiver and sway; and below the tree,
a figure empty and white radiates in the blue storm light.

Beatitude for the Meek

I can be happy, because there is an outside
world to look at, which gazes back at me.

Down low on the pavement, a black slug
edged in mustard is crossing the concrete

beside the green, wormy faeces of Canada Geese.
Drops shine on the grass blades. To fall

as rain would be relief. Don't look down
to the ground, but up to the mountain

where the wind sculpts the trees, and there
is always one stark oak at the top.

The garden gate creaks, and someone is
behind me, always behind, but

don't give in. Imagine yourself as rain.
Imagine for the rest a lucky escape.

He Has a John Clare Chin

and an eye a little uncertain of itself. Among other
children, he becomes an aspen, a breeze ruffling
the mouth. It shivers, bends, resettles

itself. And when he lies down to sleep, it
does not come easy, because a worm means
an absence in the middle of things. I could talk

all night and never soothe his confusion,
only quieted when he is running—vaulting
over earth rock water—on land kept

alive by downpours and string. I owe the world
for this boy, who knows the threading
of leaf veins, thrills at frogs, every moist,

unfurling tongue that snaps on a whir. When,
in the net, the catfish flips and writhes, he lets
it fall to slap the pond, and disappear. Already

he knows how tight and muscling the heart
can grow. The bite space in the chest—what
the worm leaves behind—is large enough

for a windy carol. Can I protect this emptiness? Can I
protect it while he grows? Can I fill
this space? Can I keep it green?

Tree with Cut Limb

If only people were trees, I might like them better.
GEORGIA O'KEEFFE

How a human being is very like a chestnut tree, arms & hair
stirring like branches in the breeze, & a voice

like the susurration of leaves. I am quiet
as a dryad, & I think as a tree thinks, not with a brain

but with every part of me. I am speaking & smiling
with my whole body; but if a tree moves, you hardly notice.

My Last Beatitude

Until I had children, no one told me
that not all of them survive, that some die
along the way. No one mentioned that the womb
teeters. They didn't predict that I would sit each week
in a leather hospital chair: strapped to a fetal monitor, I
waited for the tiny roar of the baby's heartbeat. The foetus
lay under a mountain, my body not the haven I hoped for,
but a betrayal pulsing oxygen down the measly umbilical. No
one knew that, during the birth, a shrill alarm would palpitate
while the doctor and nurses gathered. I wish I could say that
when you were born, I was glad, but at first, I felt only fear.
Your eyes narrowed, accused me as you howled. No one
said peace would happen this way: stealing on me, you
already long: we lay awake, knowing each other
so well. Nobody said how close a mother
and baby could be: as close
as teeth in the same
mouth.

Hand & Skull

'This hand reaching

     for warmth—does

          anyone

ever
     find it?

This hand

       (finding only

bone) reaches

    to tell you—

          good

          -night.'

NOTES

The Welsh phrases from **Blind Horse Elegy** come from *Pedeir Keinc Y Mabinogi* (1951, ed. Ifor Williams), and they were brought to my attention by Jenni Rowland's article in *Cambrian Medieval Celtic Studies* (63) on 'The Maiming of Horses in "Branwen"'. The Welsh in the poem in translated by Rowland as: 'Then he fell upon the horses and cut their lips from their teeth and their ears from their heads'; 'Is that what they have done concerning so good a maiden as she and my sister?'

Poem for Emily Doe is a found poem, which adapts and paraphrases testimony from a witness, 'Emily Doe', in the People of the State of California v. Brock Allen Turner (2015). 'Sonnet for the Hole in the Glass' and 'Beatitudes for the Women' draw on a number of other legal cases including the State of Oklahoma versus Daniel Holtzclaw (2016); India versus Ram Singh and Others (2014); and Regina (UK) versus Chedwyn Michael Evans and Clayton Rodney McDonald (2016); as well as Amnesty International's 2005 report: 'Stonewalled: Police abuse and misconduct against LGBT people in the US'.

Rare quotes Georgia O'Keeffe in its opening lines. 'Letter from Georgia O'Keeffe', 'Hand & Breast' and 'Hand & Bone' paraphrase O'Keeffe's sayings and moments from her letters to Alfred Stieglitz featured in the volume *My Faraway One*. 'Tree with Cut Limb' quotes Waldo Frank's description of O'Keeffe in the essay 'White Paint and Good Order'.

Syringe takes its first line from the beginning of James Merrill's 'Syrinx' and its last line from the end of John Ashbery's 'Syringa'.

Letter from Edna Pontellier applies OULIPO techniques to passages from Kate Chopin's *The Awakening*, and 'Letter from Nemi' paraphrases the firework scene from Muriel Sparks' novel *The Takeover*.

Eagle Poem and **Name Poem** are elaborations of Marina Tsvetaeva's 'No One Has Taken Anything Away' and 'Poem for Blok'. The epigraph to 'Eagle Poem' is taken from the suicide note she left for her son Mur.

My Last Beatitude refers to lyrics from Beethoven's song cycle *An die ferne Geliebte*, 'To the distant Beloved' ('Where the Mountains are So Blue').

ACKNOWLEDGEMENTS

These poems have appeared or are forthcoming in:

USA: *About Place, Chicago Review, Copper Nickel, The Hopper, Orion, Permafrost, The Manhattan Review, Mothers Always Write, Rattle, So to Speak* and *The Tahoma Literary Review*;

IRELAND & NORTHERN IRELAND: *The Honest Ulsterman, The Moth, Poetry Ireland Review* and *Abridged*;

ENGLAND & WALES: *Agenda, Compass, The New European, Magma, Poetic Interviews, Poetry Wales, Planet: the Welsh Internationalist, The New Welsh Review*, and the anthologies *Hallelujah for 50ft Women: poems about women's relationships to their bodies* (Bloodaxe Books, 2015) and *The Edge of Necessary: Welsh Innovative Poetry 1966-2018* (Aquifer Books, 2018).

AUSTRALIA: *Australian Book Review* and *Writing from Below*;

'Dryad' appeared in the art exhibition *Elemental Dialogues* at Winchester Arts Centre, England in 2014. 'Dryad' was also published in an early form on the *Against Rape* blog, an anti-sexual-violence campaign curated by Michelle McGrane.

'Sonnet for the Hole in the Glass won the Rattle Ekphrastic Challenge, winner of the Editor's Choice (October 2017). Poems from this collection also appeared in the chapbook *Blind Horse Elegy* (Oxford: Poetry Annals, 2018). Poems included here were also shortlisted or finalists for the Brittingham and Felix Pollak Prize, the Oberlin FIELD Prize, Autumn House Books Prize, C&R Press Summer Tidepool Series, Coal Hill Chapbook Competition, Concrete Wolf Competition, the Hopper Poetry Prize and the Rick Campbell Prize.

Alfred Stieglitz: 'Georgia O'Keeffe, Hands and Horse Skull' (1931) on page 9: Gelatin silver print, 19.2 x 24 cm. Gift of Georgia O'Keeffe, through the generosity of The Georgia O'Keeffe Foundation and Jennifer and Joseph Duke, 1997 (1997.61.37). New York, Metropolitan Museum of Art. © 2018. Image copyright The Metropolitan Museum of Art/Art Resource/Scala, Florence.

THANKS

Love and thanks are sent to a divine quartet of American readers: Carrie Etter, Kathy Fagan, Joanna Klink and Maggie Smith. I also thank my British readers/editors: Andy Brown, Dai George, David Morley and George Ttoouli: thank you for the criticism, and for the encouragement.

Thank you to my collaborator, artist Victoria Brookland, for our long and sympathetic friendship, and to my editor Neil Astley for his unwavering patience and kindness.

Thank you to all the students I taught on Sexuality Studies 5620: Sexuality and Violence at the Ohio State University. I bear in mind (from our classes) that the legacy of violence 'is broad but not infinite' (Ann Cahill). Particular thanks to Cade Leebron and Jackie Hedeman for helping me see what is possible.

Thank you to Sara Lee-ling Chan (then at the Tate, London) for help researching Georgia O'Keeffe. Thanks to Gayle Strege for access to the Historic Costume & Textiles Collection at the Ohio State University.

This book was completed as part of the research project *Bodies in Transit 2: Difference and Indifference*, funded by the Spanish Ministry of Education and Universities, Ref. FFI2017-84555-C2-2-P.